EUREKA!

THE BIOGRAPHY OF AN IDEA!

T0385547

WIND POWER

BY LAURA DRISCOLL • ILLUSTRATED BY BY MARCO GUADALUPI

KANEPRESS

AN IMPRINT OF ASTRA BOOKS FOR YOUNG READERS

New York

For Dad —L.D.

To all children, they're our future. —M.G.

Special thanks to Sandra Harris, Executive Director,
the American Windmill Museum

Kane Press
An imprint of Astra Books for Young Readers, a division of Astra Publishing House
kanepress.com
Printed in China

Library of Congress Cataloging-in-Publication Data

Names: Driscoll, Laura, author. | Guadalupi, Marco, illustrator.
Title: Wind power / by Laura Driscoll ; illustrated by Marco Guadalupi.
Description: New York : Kane Press, an imprint of Astra Books for Young Readers, [2023] | Series:
Eureka! : the biography of an idea | Audience: Ages 4-8 | Audience: Grades K-1 | Summary: "People
have harnessed the power of the wind for thousands of years, to travel by sailboat, to cool homes,
to grind grain into flour, and even to make music. But when someone hooked a wind mill to a
generator, wind went electric, unlocking the secret to a clean, renewable energy source!
Wind Power is an entertaining and informative look at the development of an idea
with huge benefits for a greener future. This STEAM nonfiction title is part of
the Eureka! series, with each book focusing on one groundbreaking,
world-changing discovery that millions of people use every single
day"—Provided by publisher.
Identifiers: LCCN 2022007629 (print) | LCCN 2022007630 (ebook) |
  ISBN 9781662670046 (hardcover) | ISBN 9781662670022 (paperback) |
  ISBN 9781662670039 (epub)
Subjects: LCSH: Wind power—Juvenile literature.
Classification: LCC TJ820 .D75 2023 (print) | LCC TJ820 (ebook) | DDC
  621.31/2136--dc23/eng/20220523
LC record available at https://lccn.loc.gov/2022007629

10 9 8 7 6 5 4 3 2 1

iT IS A POWERFUL FORCE YOU CAN'T SEE.

It can turn your umbrella inside out. It can keep a kite up in the air. It can blow rooftops off buildings or help plants spread their seeds.

What is it?

Wind!

Wind is moving air. The air around the Earth is heated by the sun, but not evenly. Warm air tends to rise. It leaves a space and cooler air moves in to fill it. This movement of air is happening somewhere on Earth, all the time. This is wind.

WARM AIR RISING

Sometimes wind is a gentle breeze. Sometimes it is very fast and strong.

COOL AIR FALLING

AROUND 3000 BCE

Long ago, people figured out how to capture and use wind power.

Ancient Egyptians attached square sails to boats. By catching the wind, they could sail against the current in the Nile River.

AROUND 1500 BCE

Pacific Islanders built sailboats that could travel far across the ocean! The triangle sails could be tilted and turned to catch more wind.

Over time, sailors around the world tried different sail shapes and added more sails.

AROUND 1000 BCE

In the deserts of Persia and Egypt, builders found a clever way to use wind power—to cool homes! They built special air vents into the rooftops.

The vents look like towers, but they catch the cool breeze and funnel it down into the building. Hotter air is forced out. In English, the vents are called **wind catchers**. Wind catchers are still in use today in many hot parts of the world.

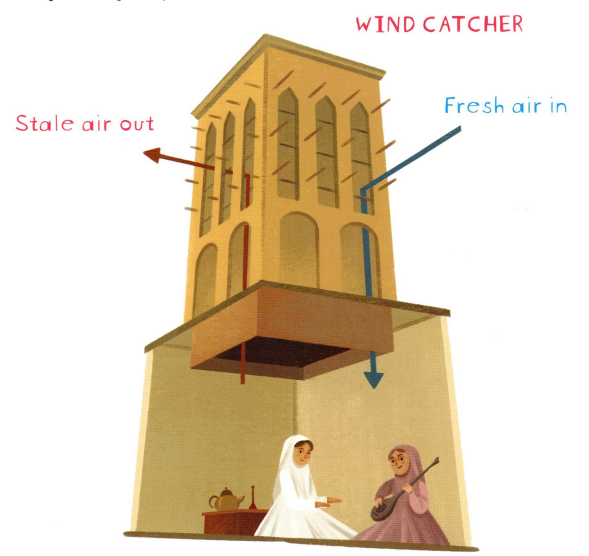

WIND CATCHER

Stale air out

Fresh air in

1ST CENTURY CE

By the year 50 CE, people were thinking of more ways to use wind. Hero, a Greek inventor, drew a plan for a wind-powered musical instrument.

In the plan, wind turned a **windwheel**. The turning motion of the wheel pushed down on an arm. The arm squished the air in a cylinder and through organ pipes to make music!

900s

A windwheel is part of another wind-powered machine: the windmill. A windmill grinds grain into flour.

In Persia, the first windmills were built in a row on top of high walls. Reed or cloth panels were attached to a center pole. The wind blew, spinning the panels around like a revolving door. The center pole rotated, turning a heavy stone underneath. The stone ground the wheat into flour.

People used the flour to make bread.

1100s

Windmills in Europe looked different. They had four sails to catch the wind. The windmill was built around a single post. If the wind changed direction? No problem! The whole windmill could be turned to face another way.

1600s To 1800s

Eventually there were up to 200,000 windmills in Europe. They ground wheat, corn, barley, and rice. They ground olives into olive oil. Some ground old ropes into pulp to make paper, or flax seeds to make linen cloth.

Around the world, wind was helping to do the work of thousands of people.

HOW A WINDMILL WORKS

Here comes a breeze!

The wind turns the **sails** of the windmill.
As the sails spin,
the **wind shaft** turns,
making **cogwheels** turn,
and the **upright shaft**, too.
Finally, the upright shaft turns the **grind wheels**.
Under the wheels, the wheat is crushed into flour.
The flour
f
a
l
l
s
through chutes,
into sacks.

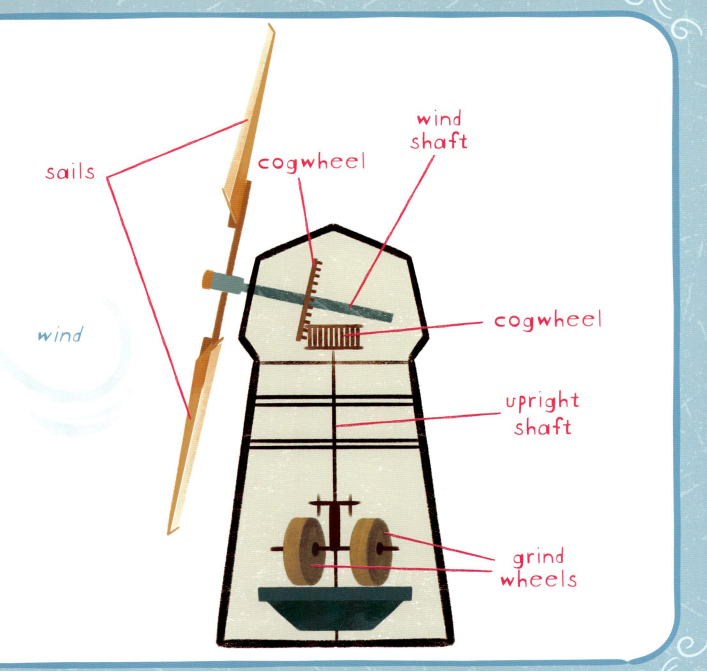

sails

wind

cogwheel

wind shaft

cogwheel

upright shaft

grind wheels

1853

By the 1800s, wind was doing a lot of work. What else could it do? Could it . . . help people fly?

Kites had been around for 5,000 or even 10,000 years. British inventor George Cayley used the same idea to build a gliding plane. It didn't need any fuel because it had no engine!

1887

Wind power took a huge jump forward when it got electric!

A Scottish professor named James Blyth added a simple electric generator to a windmill. The windmill spun parts of the generator. Inside, coils of wire moved past magnets, making electricity! Blyth used it to power the lights in his cottage.

This was the world's first wind turbine. Wind turbines turn wind energy into electricity.

Still, in the 1900s, coal was used more widely than wind power. When burned, coal gives off energy. But it also pollutes the air.

Not wind! Unlike coal, wind power is
clean and also renewable. That means the Earth
can't run out of it.

1980s TO PRESENT

Wind turbines have gotten a lot bigger. Today they are 300 feet tall, about the size of the Statue of Liberty. And that's not including the length of the blades!

Wind turbines are often grouped together in windy places. These are called wind farms. One wind farm can make electricity for thousands of homes.

Some people worry that birds and bats may fly into the wind farms and get hurt. So scientists place wind farms carefully to avoid birds' busy travel routes.

Clean energy sources like wind power are better for all of Earth's creatures than burning coal or oil.

What will wind power be like in the future? Flying wind turbines may make use of the stronger winds high in the sky. They could be floated using a gas like helium. Or they could be attached to a large kite.

New kinds of wind-powered ships might join sailboats on the oceans. On some, the sails would look more like airplane wings. On others, giant kites tied to the ships would help pull them along.

With every new use of wind power, we can burn less of other fuels. That's good for the planet and for our future.

So the next time the wind blows over your beach umbrella,
just remember all the wonderful things the wind can do!

WHEN THE WIND BLOWS

• Most windmills and wind turbines spin clockwise. But early windmills turned the opposite way!

• Charles Brush built the first American wind turbine in his backyard in 1888.

• Anemometers measure wind speed. On Earth, the highest wind gust speed ever recorded was 253 miles per hour.

• Earth doesn't have the strongest winds in our solar system. Saturn and Neptune do! Wind there can reach more than 1,000 miles per hour.

• In 1925, Frenchman Georges Darrieus invented a wind turbine that looked like a giant eggbeater.

• Today's gliders can stay in the air for hours—even days! In 1961, two men kept their plane aloft for 71 hours.

• Close to the Earth's equator is a nearly windless area called the doldrums. Sometimes sailing ships got stuck there for weeks!

WINDY DAYS

The **Beaufort Scale** describes wind speed, with ratings from 0 to 12.
So 2 is a light breeze and "leaves rustle." 10 is a storm with "trees uprooted."

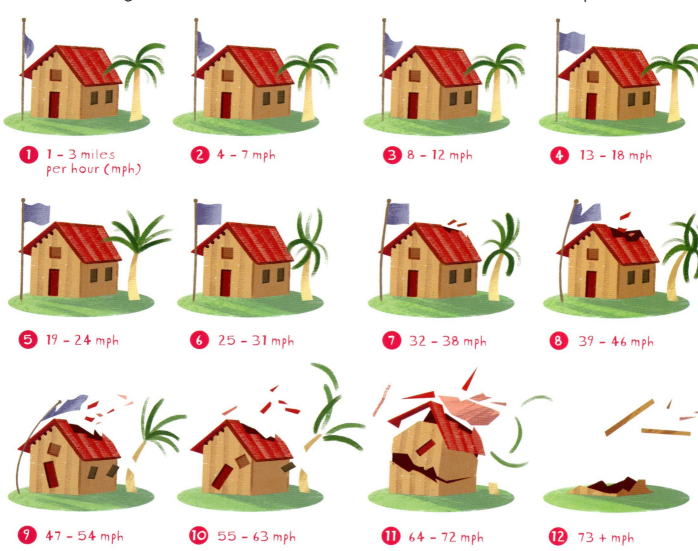

1. 1 – 3 miles per hour (mph)
2. 4 – 7 mph
3. 8 – 12 mph
4. 13 – 18 mph
5. 19 – 24 mph
6. 25 – 31 mph
7. 32 – 38 mph
8. 39 – 46 mph
9. 47 – 54 mph
10. 55 – 63 mph
11. 64 – 72 mph
12. 73 + mph